Jorge Manrique

Titles in the *Shearsman Classics* series:

1. *Poets of Devon and Cornwall, from Barclay to Coleridge* (2007)
2. Robert Herrick *Selected Poems* (2007)
3. *Spanish Poetry of the Golden Age, in contemporary English translations* (2008)
4. Mary, Lady Chudleigh *Selected Poems* (2009)
5. William Strode *Selected Poems* (2009)
6. Sir Thomas Wyatt *Selected Poems* (2010)
7. *Tottel's Miscellany* (1557) (The Tudor Miscellanies, Vol. 1) (2010)
8. *The Phœnix Nest* (1593) (The Tudor Miscellanies, Vol. 2) (2010)
9. *Englands Helicon* (1600) (The Tudor Miscellanies, Vol. 3) (2010)
10. Mary Coleridge *Selected Poems* (2010)
11. D.H. Lawrence *Look! We Have Come Through!* (2011)
12. D.H. Lawrence *Birds, Beasts and Flowers* (2011)
13. D.H. Lawrence *Studies in Classic American Literature* (2011)
14. Johann Wolfgang von Goethe *Faust* (translated by Mike Smith) (2012)
15. Robert Browning *Dramatic Romances* (2012)
16. Robert Browning *Sordello* (2012)
17. Robert Browning *The Ring and the Book* (2012)
18. Fernando de Herrera *Selected Poems*
          (translated by Luis Ingelmo & Michael Smith) (2014)
19. Thomas Gray *The English Poems* (2014)
20. Antonio Machado *Solitudes & Other Early Poems*
          (translated by Michael Smith & Luis Ingelmo) (2015)
21. John Donne *Poems (1633)* (2015)
22. Thomas Carew *Collected Poems* (2015)
23. Gerard Manley Hopkins *The Wreck of the Deutschland* (ed. Foxell) (2017)
24. Gérard de Nerval *Les Chimères* (translated by Will Stone) (2017)
25. Sir John Suckling *Collected Poems* (2020)
26. Richard Lovelace *Collected Poems* (2020)
27. Robert Herrick *Hesperides (1648)* (2018)
28. Algernon Charles Swinburne *Our Lady of Pain: Poems of Eros and
          Perversion* (edited by Mark Scroggins) (2019)
29. Luís Vaz de Camões *The Lusiads*
          (translated by Sir Richard Fanshawe, 1655) (2021)
30. Luís Vaz de Camões *Selected Shorter Poems*
          (translated by Jonathan Griffin) (2021)
31. Rubén Darío *Selected Poems* (translated by Adam Feinstein) (2020)
32. Jorge Manrique *Stanzas on the Death of His Father* (translated by
          Patrick McGuinness) (2021)

Jorge Manrique

Stanzas on the Death of His Father

Coplas a la muerte de su padre

translated from the Spanish by
Patrick McGuinness

with an introduction by Geraldine Hazbun

Shearsman Classics

First published in the United Kingdom in 2021 by
Shearsman Books
PO Box 4239
Swindon
SN3 9FN

Shearsman Books Ltd Registered Office
30–31 St. James Place, Mangotsfield, Bristol BS16 9JB
(this address not for correspondence)

www.shearsman.com

Shearsman Classics Vol. 32

ISBN 978-1-84861-772-8

Contents

Introduction   7

Coplas a la muerte de su padre   16

Translator's Note   99

Acknowledgements   101

In memory of our student, Rebecca Henderson,
scholar and medievalist, 1994–2019

G.H.
P.McG.

Coplas a la muerte de su padre

Coplas a la muerte de su padre by Jorge Manrique (c.1440–79) is one of the most celebrated poems in the Spanish language. Written shortly before the poet's death, it is a dignified elegy that speaks not just of a personal loss, that of the poet's father Rodrigo Manrique (d.1476), but of the evanescence of all things *sub specie aeternitatis*. Its popularity is aided by memorable lines, not least the two opening metaphors: man's life is a river meandering unto the sea of death (st. 3), and this world is the road to the next, the lasting dwelling place (st. 5). The poem replicates these reflections in its wending form. Its forty stanzas each comprise four tercets; each tercet is made up of two longer octosyllabic verses combined with one four-syllable half-line known as *pie quebrado*. These regular broken lines, like beats of a heart, invest the poem with a resonant quality befitting the injunction at the opening of the poem to awaken one's slumbering soul to the passage of time: 'Recuerde el alma dormida, | avive el seso e despierte' (st. 1). The poetic structure is supported by an overarching conceptual one, that of the three lives – the physical life, the life of *fama* (a posthumous reputation for remarkable deeds), and the eternal life of heaven. To this Christian Neo-Stoic view of life and death, Manrique adds his own touch. Time is entirely relative, everything is precarious and imminent: what is being said is already spoken, what is at its height is already at its point of decline. Throughout the poem we are exposed repeatedly to the conjoined nature of human experience. Manrique's masterstroke – aided by repetition, antonyms, conjunctions, parallels, and other forms of aesthetic chicanery – is to tread the borderline between life and death precisely, keeping the reader at a point where death constantly intrudes on life and life is a perpetual state of near-death. In Christian tradition this is a widely recognized crossover, not least in the presence of Christ on earth, a fact alluded to in the poem, but also in the thought of St Augustine, whose vision of the two cities, the City of God and the City of Man, turned human life into a living pilgrimage towards heaven.

Jorge Manrique came from an exemplary aristocratic background. The family were old Castilian nobility of the Lara dynasty and came to be closely involved in the turbulent political scene surrounding the reigns of Juan II (1406-54) and Enrique IV (1425–74). Jorge's grandfather Pedro Manrique was *adelantado* (governor) of León and married Leonor of Castile, granddaughter of Enrique II. Jorge's father Rodrigo was a towering figure of the fifteenth-century reconquest, a reputation founded on his military campaigns at the frontier. When he was twelve he was made a knight of the Order of Santiago, a military order established in 1171 for the purpose of fighting the Moors in Iberia and protecting pilgrims to Santiago de Compostela. According to his biography in Fernando de Pulgar's *Claros varones de Castilla*, his name struck terror into the kingdom of Granada, last bastion of Moorish Spain. Celebrated among the Christians as a brave and brilliant knight, Rodrigo was honoured by King Juan II as Count of Paredes and elected Master of the Order of Santiago. Jorge Manrique's uncle, Gómez Manrique, was also a distinguished figure. A highly respected court poet and dramatist, he was *corregidor* (magistrate) of Toledo for fourteen years, an appointment possibly connected to his support for Isabel and Fernando, the Catholic Monarchs. As for Jorge Manrique, he too was actively involved in the political affairs of his time, often acting alongside his father for the cause of Isabel and Fernando. He became a captain of the Santa Hermandad (Holy Brotherhood) of Toledo in the later stages of his life and, as a result of military action at the castle of Garcimuñoz, died from an injury to the groin in April 1479.

The tumultuous politics of the fifteenth century provides both context and content for Manrique's *Coplas*. When he writes of the vanishing glories of the court, when he asks what has become of the jousts, the plumes, the tournaments, the flags and the horses, he does so as someone familiar with this setting, someone for whom chivalry is not a fantasy but a way of life. What more appropriate material could there be for an elegy on a transitory life than the rise and fall of nobles and kings in a century during which Fortune's wheel was notoriously indiscriminate and the fabric of society was changing? Manrique's imagery is both literal and referential, a confluence of real people and objects and their symbolic potential, in keeping with his union of the particular and the universal in the poem more broadly. The Coplas are tripartite, beginning with general reflections on mortality (ss. 1–13), followed by a section of negative *exempla* (ss. 14-24), then culminating in praise of Rodrigo's exceptional life and achievements (ss. 25-40). Within the first section, the opening stanzas stress cognition, inviting man to awaken, to remember, to see, to think, and to judge (*recordar, despertar, ver, juzgar, pensar*) the reality of life passing and death making its stealthy approach. Verbs such as these are a staple of the literature of the Spanish Golden Age, that period famed for its obsession with the concepts of being and seeming (*ser / parecer*), of trickery and disillusion (*engaño / desengaño*). Manrique's is also a world of false appearances, although not yet tinged with the bitterness one might associate with that later period, and writers such as Quevedo. A posture of contempt for the world certainly emerges in these early stanzas; it is a treacherous 'mundo traidor' (st. 8), a world that was blind to Christ ('el mundo non conoció su deidad' [st. 4]), and a trap, 'la çelada | en que caemos' (st. 13). However, it is still a hopeful road to the next life (st. 5), a world that can serve us well if we use it well, 'Este mundo bueno fue | si bien usásemos dél | como debemos' (st. 6), and a world in which the son of God lived amongst men for their salvation (st. 6). Manrique's particular brand of *desengaño* focuses more on time, and its relativity. When he invites us to consider the future as already past, 'daremos lo no venido por passado' (st. 2), he compresses past, present, and future together in such a way as to illustrate that no pleasure can endure and therein lies the rub: 'Non se engañe nadi, no' (st. 2). Do not be fooled, he warns, for life passes like a dream, 'se va la vida apriessa como sueño' (st.

12). Complementing this accelerated vision of time is the image of Fortune's wheel, an age-old motif which he makes his own by stressing the imminence of its turning; if the future is already the past, material achievements like 'estados e riqueza' are also, at one and the same time the property of Fortune: 'bienes ... de Fortuna | que revuelven con su rueda' (st. 11).

In the second section of the *Coplas*, Manrique turns to more concrete examples of the transitory nature of worldly affairs, but not before introducing a couple of corporeal illustrations in section one. The first is that of the physical body, of human beauty and strength becoming old and cumbersome (st. 9). This is followed by a reference to the sullying of the 'sangre de los godos' (st. 10), the noble blood of the Visigoths. This is developed with greater specificity in the second section where Manrique lists historical examples of great men who have been brought low, warning that death is indiscriminate; that no pope, emperor, nor prelate can escape its levelling effect, a key element in the Dance of Death tradition. The Trojans, Romans, and ancient 'reyes poderosos' are dispensed with summarily in favour of more recent examples. Let us deal with yesterday, suggests Manrique, 'vengamos a lo d'ayer', since that too is forgotten, 'que también es olvidado | como aquello' (st. 15). His point here is that *olvido* is an absolute; the recent past is still essentially the past; the experience of fallen greatness is close at hand and it simply is not necessary to travel back to the classical world to find it. The ensuing list of mighty characters from recent history provides further evidence of the compression of time Manrique presents. This gives the *ubi sunt* (where are they now?) *topos* a particular inflection. Instead of dredging up memories of the ancients, we experience the unsettling reminder that those of recent political distinction have also departed, and are also subject to the vicissitudes of memory. Manrique's version of the *ubi sunt* is remarkably fluid. What could be a brittle rhetorical question becomes an exercise in simultaneously revelling in the glories and greatness of court, and establishing the court as an *exemplum* of mutability. His questions shift perspective: ¿qué se hizo / hizieron…? (what did he/ they do?), ¿Qué fue de (what has become of?) (st. 16), ¿Qué fueron? (what were they?) (st. 19, 21), ¿dónde iremos a buscallos? (where shall we find them?) (st. 19). There is, however, an overarching interest in doing and being, *hazer* and *ser*, in keeping with Manrique's conviction that good deeds in this life secure *fama* after death. The cast of characters held up in this section as examples of the transitory nature of worldly power could be alienating for a modern day reader without a history book at hand, but for Manrique's audience this represented the fifteenth century court in all its might and intrigue. In descending order of eminence, and starting with the oldest examples, Manrique first lists kings and princes—Juan II of Castile (1406–54), the Infantes of Aragón, Enrique IV of Castile (1454–74), Prince Alfonso – then the powerful court favourites Álvaro de Luna (Constable of Castile and favourite of Juan II), Juan Pacheco and Pedro Téllez Girón (favourites of Enrique IV), then a generic group of dukes, marquises, counts, and noblemen. Finally, he alludes to troops, pennants, standards, flags, impregnable castle, walls, ramparts, and trenches. From the king's body – the true body politic – we move through a series of substitutes and versions; princes and heirs, favourites (who often operated in the king's place), and the nobility. In a form of synecdoche, or perhaps it is also bathos, we then reach the material objects that mount a futile defence of the crown in the face of death's piercing arrow, '¿qué aprovecha? | Cuando tú vienes airada, | todo lo passas de claro | con tu flecha' (st. 24). This is a conceit in death literature, that no human defence can stand up to death, but here it is also a prescient observation of a chivalric ideal that is already crumbling.

The third and final section is reserved for Rodrigo Manrique. Where all other defences fail, Rodrigo retains the status of 'abrigo', a shelter for the good (st. 25). Against the backdrop of a world of disappearing greatness, he is described in a language of light and vision. In a further example of how relevant the exemplary value of the recent past is, Rodrigo's illustrious deeds, 'hechos grandes e claros' stand for all to see, 'pues los vieron' (st. 25). This is a gesture towards the *claros varones* tradition, a literary tendency developed from humanistic Latin tradition which created brief biographical summaries of illustrious historical figures, its chief examples in Castile being Fernán Pérez de Guzmán's *Generaciones y semblanzas* and Hernando del Pulgar's *Claros varones de Castilla*. Rodrigo is duly enshrined in this tradition but retains an important proximity, close enough to the audience to be described with the demonstrative pronoun 'Aquel [de buenos abrigo]' (st. 25). We may recall Manrique's earlier rejection of examples from written history, 'escripturas | ya passadas' (st. 14). All the world, we are told, knows what Rodrigo's deeds are 'el mundo todo sabe | cuáles fueron' (st. 25); it is as if the poet doesn't need to describe them, although he does go on to do so. Manrique's *encomium* of his father is understandably hyperbolic, testing the limits of both language and exemplarity with a strong anaphoric 'qué': '¡qué señor para criados […] Qué maestro d'esforçados' (st. 26), and with recursive and parallelistic techniques; '¡Amigo de su amigos […] enemigo d'enemigos!' (st. 26). The ensuing stanzas, where Manrique likens his father to the Roman emperors, may come as something of a surprise in a poem that sets its store by the recent past. In fact, critics have considered these the worst stanzas in the poem. The presence of Roman history is, however, an important connection with Castile's chronicle tradition, especially the works of Alfonso X el Sabio (1252–84), whose chronicles are a likely source for these stanzas. Alfonso holds Roman history up as the supreme example of the transitory nature of political greatness, of the fall of empire. This makes it a fitting prelude in the poem to Rodrigo's military campaigns against the Moors, which are elevated to comparable heights of political merit, and spiritual worth, as Rodrigo renounces the vanities and treasures of the world for the tangible conquests of Moorish towns and fortresses: 'Non dexó grandes tesoros, | ni alcançó muchas riquezas | ni vaxillas; | mas fizo guerra a los moros' (st. 29). For all Manrique's emphasis on the recent past, it seems he does not reject more distant history outright. The old stories are rewritten by his father for his own time: 'Estas sus viejas hestorias [...] con otras nuevas victorias | agora las renovó en senectud' (st. 31). Manrique also uses a lexis befitting Roman history; Rodrigo reconquered towns and lands from 'tiranos', recovering them for his 'rey natural' (st. 31), where the adjective 'natural' taps into a central part of Alfonso X's political philosophy – that the king is the natural / organic leader of his people and that the bond between them is pre-ordained and mutual, a feeling echoed in the description of him serving his 'rey verdadero' (st. 33).

By stanza 33, Rodrigo has played the game of war, served the crown, and words can no longer suffice: 'que non puede bastar cuenta cierta'. At this point in the poem, Death comes knocking at Rodrigo's door, imbuing the poem with the imminence we have come to associate with death, but also with a performative quality. In the personification of death, there appears to be a connection with the Dance of Death or *Danza de la muerte*, although it is not certain that this is a direct one; it may just be a case of common conventions about death in the fifteenth century. Unlike the character of death in the *Danza*, a grim leveller associated with the macabre aspects of dying, Death in the *Coplas* ushers Rodrigo from the transitory life on earth, via the second life of 'la fama gloriosa' (st. 35), to the third and lasting life of heaven, a life he has won in the only way a Christian knight can: the spilling of pagan blood in 'trabajos e aflicciones | contra moros' (st. 36). To a modern reader this may be an uncomfortable triumph, but it is important to guard against anachronism and exaggeration on this point. Rodrigo was engaged in the work of a fifteenth-century Castilian knight – recovering land from the Moors and fighting at the frontier; there is no escaping that. However, the poem reads more like aristocratic/chivalric, than religious, propaganda. Although the poem is infused with Christian belief and doctrine it is less a rallying call to arms, and more a wistful reflection on proven military triumph and family achievement at a time when the old orders were starting to break down, exacerbated by rifts between aristocracy and crown, and near-constant civil strife in fifteenth-century Castile. The tangible gains of Rodrigo, evident in the emphasis on 'ganar' and 'galardón' in stanza 37, contrast with a social order that was no longer as favourable to the nobility, and was starting to erode the influence of Manrique's very own clan and caste. In this light, the poem's earlier use of the *ubi sunt* takes on a protective, introspective air. Estate and opulence, 'estados e riqueza' (st. 11) are not expected to endure, so a more lasting achievement is called for, hence the enshrining of Rodrigo's military career in heaven. Rodrigo's response to death is pure acquiescence, so much so that he reasons that to want to live when God wishes you to die is madness (st. 38). This expression of contempt for the world, 'esta vida mesquina' (st. 38), is both deeply Christian and pragmatic. When the present is so volatile, why not look forward to securing a stable legacy at last? Rodrigo speaks next to Jesus, appealing to his clemency to ask for forgiveness, an essential element in a good death. The final stanza of the *Coplas* contains further evidence that Rodrigo is dying in the best possible way, surrounded by his wife, children, brothers, and protégés, and with all his cognitive faculties intact. Dying in the most fitting circumstances possible is linked to the *Ars moriendi* (*Art of Dying Well*), two Latin texts from the fifteenth century on the protocol of a good Christian death.

The final stanza focuses, as we might expect, on what has gone and what is left behind, concentrated in the much-quoted lines: 'aunque la vida perdió, | dexónos harto consuelo su memoria' (st. 40). There is a risk of seeing this as a platitude, like the kind of glib reflection one might find inside a condolence card, but consolation and memory here need to be understood in the context of the poet's earlier emphasis on the value of cognition: seeing, waking, remembering, judging, thinking. These are the active processes that cut through the falseness and vanity of the world, and which operate at the very boundary between life and death. 'Memoria' is not a static legacy as its rather finite placement might suggest; it is the poem's very engine, inviting the reader to participate in practices of reconstruction and imagination. The memory of Rodrigo offers no single, extractable meaning, nor does the *Coplas* itself, which instead offers up visions of the roads, routes, and pathways that might take us some way to understanding the precariousness of human life and experience, much like medieval memory itself did.

Geraldine Hazbun
Oxford

Geraldine Hazbun is Professor of Medieval Spanish Literature at Oxford and Ferreras Willetts Fellow in Spanish at St Anne's College. She works on literature from the medieval and early modern periods with particular focus on epic poetry, ballads, chronicles, and travel writing. Recent publications include *Reading Illegitimacy in Early Iberian Literature* (2020), *Narratives of the Islamic Conquest from Medieval Spain* (2015) and *Treacherous Foundations: Betrayal and Collective Identity in Early Spanish Epic, Chronicle, and Drama* (2009).

Coplas

a la muerte de su padre

Stanzas

On the Death of His Father

[I]

Recuerde el alma dormida,
abive el seso y despierte
    contemplando
cómo se pasa la vida,
cómo se viene la muerte
    tan callando;
cuánd presto se va el plazer,
cómo después de acordado
    da dolor,
cómo a nuestro parescer
cualquiera tiempo pasado
    fue mejor.

[1]

Let the sleeping soul remember,
let the mind awake and come alive,
    by contemplating
how life passes,
how death takes us
    by surprise;
how quickly pleasure fades,
how, remembering what pleasure was,
    it gives us pain;
how to our eyes
the time that's passed
    was best.

[II]

Y pues vemos lo presente
cómo en un punto se es ido
    y acabado,
si juzgamos sabiamente,
daremos lo no venido
    por pasado.

No se engañe nadie, no,
pensando que a de durar
    lo que espera
más que duró lo que vio,
porque todo ha de pasar
    por tal manera.

[II]

For when we see the present,
how in a moment
     it is gone,
if we judge things wisely
we will treat what is to come
     as if it were already past.
No, we are not wrong
to think that what
     we hope to see
will last no longer than what we saw,
since everything is bound to pass
     this way.

[III]

Nuestras vidas son los ríos
que van a dar en el mar
  que es el morir:
allí van los señoríos
derechos a se acabar
  y consumir;
allí, los ríos caudales,
allí, los otros, medianos,
  y más chicos;
allegados, son iguales,
los que biven por sus manos
  y los ricos.

[III]

Our lives are the rivers
that flow down to the sea
  that dying is;
there flow the Lordships,
down to their ends
  to be consumed;
there flow the great rivers,
and there, the others: the tributaries
  and the lesser streams;
all arrive together equal,
those who live by their hands
  and the rich.

[IV]

Dexo las invocaciones
de los famosos poetas
          y oradores;
no curo de sus ficiones,
que traen yervas secretas
          sus sabores.
A aquel solo me encomiendo,
a aquel solo invoco yo
          de verdad,
que en este mundo biviendo,
el mundo no conosció
          su deidad.

[IV]

    I disdain the invocations
of the famous poets
       and orators;
I do not care for their fictions,
they taste of spells and magic herbs;
       I entrust myself only
to the One,
I invoke only
       the One
who in this world lived
and was not known
       Divine.

[V]

Este mundo es el camino
para el otro, que es morada
    sin pesar,
mas cumple tener buen tino
para andar esta jornada
    sin errar.
Partimos cuando nascemos,
andamos cuando bivimos
    y allegamos
al tiempo que fenescemos;
así que, cuando morimos,
    descansamos.

[V]

This world is the path
that leads us to that other, our dwelling
        without sorrow;
but we must have good judgment
to make this journey
        and not lose our way.
We set out when we are born
and all our lives we walk
        until we reach
the moment of our passing;
this is how, in dying,
        we find our rest.

[VI]

Este mundo bueno fue
si bien usáramos de él
como devemos,
porque, segúnd nuestra fe,
es para ganar aquél
que atendemos;
y aun aquel hijo de Dios,
para sobirnos al cielo,
descendió
a nascer acá entre nos
y bivir en este suelo
do murió.

[VI]

    This world will have been good
if we have used it
      as we should,
since, as our faith teaches us,
it is how we gain the one
      we seek.
And even the son of God,
to raise us up to heaven,
      came down
to be born among us
and live on this earth
      where He died.

[VII]

Si fuese en nuestro poder
tornar la cara fermosa
  corporal
como podemos hazer
el ánima gloriosa
  angelical,
¡qué diligencia tan biva
tovíéramos toda ora
  y tan presta
en componer la cativa,
dexándonos la señora
  descompuesta!

[VII]

If it lay within in our power
to make our fleshly face
      as beautiful
as we can make
our glorious soul
      angelical,
how we would strive each hour,
with what persistence,
      how willingly,
to beautify the slave,
and leave the mistress
      to decay!

[VIII]

Ved de quánd poco valor
son las cosas tras que andamos
y corremos
que, en este mundo traidor,
aun primero que muramos
las perdemos:
de ellas deshaze la hedad,
de ellas, casos desastrados
que contecen,
de ellas, por su calidad,
en los más altos estados
desfallescen.

[VIII]

See how little they are worth,
the things we strive for
    and pursue,
how in this deceitful world
they are lost to us
    even before we die:
some undone by age,
some broken by the chance disasters
    that befall them;
others by their nature perish
when they reach their
    highest state.

[IX]

Dezidme: la hermosura,
la gentil frescura y tez
        de la cara,
la color y la blancura,
cuando viene la vejez,
        ¿cuál se para?
Las mañas y ligereza
y la fuerca corporal
        de juventud,
todo se torna graveza
cuando llega al arraval
        de senetud.

[IX]

Tell me: beauty,
the sweet and fresh complexion
        of the face,
its colour and its whiteness:
what becomes of them
        when old age arrives?
As for agility and lightness,
the body's strength
        in youth,
they all turn heavy
when we reach the slum
        of our senescence.

[X]

Pues la sangre de los godos,
el linage y la nobleza
    tan crescida,
¡por cuantas vías y modos
se sume su grand alteza
    en esta vida!
Unos, por poco valer,
¡por cuánd baxos y abatidos
    que los tienen!
otros que, por no tener,
con oficios no devidos
    se sostienen.

[X]

    As for the blood of the Goths,
the lineage, the nobility
      that rose so high,
by how many means and ways
was their majesty exalted
      in this life!
Some are despised for lack of worth;
how low and base
      they are held to be!
Others, for lack of means,
maintain themselves
      with unseemly offices.

[XI]

Los estados y riqueza,
que nos dexan a desora,
¡quién lo duda!
No les pidamos firmeza,
pues que son de una señora
que se muda:
que bienes son de fortuna
que rebuelve con su rueda
presurosa,
la cual no puede ser una
ni ser estable ni queda
en una cosa.

[XI]

Our positions and our riches,
abandon us before our time,
    who can doubt it?
We cannot ask them to stand firm
for they come from a changeable
    lady;
they are gifts of Fortune
who turns so fast
    upon her wheel
that she cannot be of one mind
or remain fixed and stable
    in any single thing.

[XII]

Pero digo que acompañen
y lleguen hasta la huesa
    con su dueño:
por eso no nos engañen,
pues se va la vida apriesa
    como sueño.
Y los deleites de acá
son, en que nos deleitamos,
    temporales,
y los tormentos de allá
que por ellos esperamos,
    eternales.

[XII]

For I say though they may follow us
they end up with their owner
  in the grave:
that's why they cannot fool us,
for life goes quickly
  as a dream,
and the pleasures that so delight us
  here below
are things of Time,
while the torments that lie beyond,
and which through them await us
  are timeless.

[XIII]

Los plazeres y dulcores
de esta vida trabajada
        que tenemos
no son sino corredores,
y la muerte, la celada
        en que caemos.
No mirando a nuestro daño,
corremos a rienda suelta,
        sin parar;
cuando vemos el engaño
y queremos dar la buelta,
        no ay lugar.

[XIII]

The pleasures and the sweet things
in this toilsome life
    of ours,
what are they but vain chases,
and death the ambush
    we fall into?
We do not see the danger,
we run headlong
    and will not stop,
but when we see we have been tricked
and want to turn around
    it is too late.

[XIV]

Estos reyes poderosos
que vemos por escripturas
        ya pasadas,
con casos tristes, llorosos,
fueron sus buenas venturas
        trastornadas;
así que no ay cosa fuerte,
que a papas y emperadores
        y perlados,
así los trata la muerte
como a los pobres pastores
        de ganados.

[XIV]

Those mighty kings
we read of in the writings
        of the past,
how their lucky ventures
        were reversed;
thus nothing endures
since Death treats popes and emperors
        and prelates
as it treats the humblest herdsman
        with his sheep.

[XV]

Dexemos a los troyanos,
que sus males no los vimos
ni sus glorias;
dexemos a los romanos,
aunque oímos y leímos
sus vitorias.
No curemos de saber
lo de aquel siglo pasado
qué fue dello;
vengamos a lo de ayer,
que tan bien es olvidado
como aquéllo.

[XV]

Let us leave aside the Trojans
for we saw nothing of their suffering
or their glories;
let us leave aside the Romans,
though we listened to and read
their victories.
Let us not seek to know
of some past century
and what became of it;
let us see the things of yesterday,
how they have been, like them,
forgotten.

[XVI]

   ¿Qué se hizo el rey don Juan?
Los infantes de Aragón,
     ¿qué se hizieron?
¿Qué fue de tanto galán?
¿Qué fue de tanta invención
     como traxieron?
Las justas y los torneos,
paramentos, bordaduras
     y cimeras
¿fueron sino devaneos?
¿Qué fueron sino verduras
     de las heras?

[XVI]

What became of King Juan?
The princes of Aragon,
      what became of them?
What happened to such fine young men?
What of all the fine inventions
      they devised?
The jousting and the tournaments,
the bright embroideries, the ornaments
      and plumes;
what were they if not fancies?
What were they but the grass
      left on the threshing-floor?

[XVII]

　　¿Qué se hizieron las damas,
sus tocados, sus vestidos,
　　　sus olores?
¿Qué se hizieron las llamas
de los fuegos encendidos
　　　de amadores?
¿Qué se hizo aquel trobar,
las músicas acordadas
　　　que tañían?
¿Qué se hizo aquel dancar,
y aquellas ropas chapadas
　　　que trayani

[XVII]

What became of the Ladies,
their headdresses, their finery,
        their scents?
Where now are the flames
lit by so many lovers'
        fires?
And where now are their poems,
the tuneful music
        that they played?
Where now are their dances,
the brightly-coloured gowns
        they trailed?

[XVIII]

Pues el otro, su heredero,
don Enrique, ¡qué poderes
    alcancava!
¡Cuánd blando, cuánd balaguero,
el mundo con sus plazeres
    se le dava!
Mas verás cuánd enemigo,
cuánd contrario, cuánd cruel
    se le mostró:
aviéndole seído amigo,
¡cuánd poco duró con él
    lo que le dio!

[XVIII]

    And that other king, his heir
Don Enrique, what power
        he attained!
How sweet and promising
the world and all its pleasures
        appeared to be for him!
But you will see how contrary
an enemy this friend
        revealed itself to be,
how cruel; how briefly
it bestowed
        the gifts it gave.

[XIX]

Las dádivas desmedidas,
los hedificios reales
    llenos de oro,
las baxillas tan febridas,
los enriques y reales
    del thesoro,
los jaezes y cavallos
de su gente y atavíos
    tan sobrados
¿dónde iremos a buscallos?
¿Qué fueron sino rocíos
    de los prados?

[XIX]

The extravagant presents,
the royal palaces
    filled with gold,
the burnished tableware,
the gold and silver coins
    of the treasury;
the harnesses and horses
of his men, all that excessive
    finery,
where should we go to find them?
What were they but dewdrops
    on the fields?

[XX]

Pues su hermano el inocente,
que en su vida subcesor
    se llamó,
qué corte tan excelente
tuvo, y cuánto grand señor
    que le siguió;
mas como fuese mortal,
metióle la muerte luego
    en su fragua.
¡O juizio divinal,
cuando más ardía el fuego,
    echaste agua!

[XX]

    And what of his brother, the innocent,
who when he lived was called
       the heir;
what a sumptuous court
he had, what great lords
       followed him!
But, as he was mortal,
so death fired him
       in his forge.
O Divine judgment:
when the flames burned hottest
       you threw on water.

[XXI]

Pues aquel grand Condestable,
maestre que conoscimos
        tan privado,
no cumple que de él se hable,
sino sólo que lo vimos
        degollado;
sus infinitos tesoros,
sus villas y sus lugares,
        su mandar,
¿qué le fueron sino lloros?
¿Fuéronle sino pesares
        al dexar?

[XXI]

And the great High Constable,
the master whom we knew
        as such a favourite;
we ought not to speak of him
except to say we witnessed
        his beheading.
His immeasurable treasures,
his towns and his estates,
        his high authority,
what were they to him but tears?
What were they but the grief
        he had in leaving them?

[XXII]

Pues los otros dos hermanos,
maestres tan prosperados
    como reyes,
que a los grandes y medianos
truxeron tan sojuzgados
    a sus leyes;
aquella prosperidad
que tan alto fue subida
    y enxalcada
¿qué fue sino claridad,
que estando más encendida
    fue amatada?

[XXII]

And the other two brothers,
such wealthy masters,
    so like Kings
that the middling and the great
bowed down in subjection
    to their laws;
their vast wealth
that rose so high
    and was so exalted:
what was it but a light
that – when it burned most brightly –
    was snuffed out?

[XXIII]

Tantos duques excelentes,
tantos marqueses y condes
    y varones
como vimos tan potentes,
di, muerte, ¿dó los escondes
    y traspones?
Y sus muy claras hazañas
que hizieron en las guerras
    y en las pazes,
cuando tú, cruda, te ensañas,
con tu fuerca las atierras
    y deshazes.

[XXIII]

    All those great dukes
those marquises and counts;
       those nobles
who we saw in all their might;
tell us where you hide them, Death,
       where did you take them to?
What are their famous exploits now,
their accomplishments in war
       and peace?
When you, cruel Death, enraged,
cast them to the ground and with your strength
       destroy them.

[XXIV]

Las huestes innumerables,
los pendones y estandartes
  y vanderas,
los castillos impunables,
los muros y valuartes
  y barreras,
la cava honda, chapada,
o cualquier otro reparo
  ¿qué aprovecha?
Que si tú vienes airada
todo lo pasas de claro
  con tu frecha.

[XXIV}

The countless troops,
the pennants, the standards
        and the flags;
the impregnable castles,
the walls, the ramparts
        and the barricades;
the deep armoured ditch
or any other refuge:
        what good are they?
If, when you come in fury,
you pierce them clean through
        with your arrow.

[XXV]

Aquél de buenos abrigo,
amado por virtuoso
    de la gente,
el maestre don Rodrigo
Manrique, tanto famoso
    y tan valiente,
sus grandes hechos y claros
no cumple que los alabe,
    pues los vieron,
ni los quiero hazer caros,
pues el mundo todo sabe
    cuáles fueron.

[XXV]

And he the protector of the good,
loved for his virtues
    by his people,
the great Master Rodrigo
Manrique, so famous
    and so brave:
his great deeds so shine
there is no need to praise them
    for they were seen by all.
I have no wish to boast of them
for the whole world knows
    what they were.

[XXVI]

Amigo de sus amigos,
¡qué señor para criados
   y parientes!
¡Qué enemigo de enemigos!
¡Qué maestro de esforcados
   y valientes!
¡Qué seso para discretos!
¡Qué gracia para donosos!
      ¡Qué razón!
¡Qué benigno a los subjetos!
Y a los bravos y dañosos,
      ¡un león!

[XXVI]

What a friend to his friends!
What a master to his servants
    and his kinsmen!
What an enemy to his enemies!
What a leader to the brave
    and valiant!
What judgment for the wise!
What humour for the witty!
    What reason!
What benevolence for his subjects!
And to the unruly and the bold,
    a lion!

[XXVII]

En ventura, Otaviano,
Julio César en vencer
        y batallar;
en la virtud, Africano,
Anibal en el saber
        y trabajar;
en la bondad, un Trajano,
Tito en liberalidad
        con alegría;
en su braco, Aureliano,
Marco Atilio en la verdad
        que prometía.

[XXVII]

Octavian in his good fortune;
Caesar in his victories
    and his battles;
in his virtue, Scipio;
Hannibal in knowledge
    and determination;
in his goodness, Trajan;
Titus in generosity
    and in joy;
in the strength of his arm, Aurelian;
Marcus Atilius in the truth
    of his word.

[XXVIII]

Antonio Pío en clemencia,
Marco Aurelio en igualdad
    del semblante;
Adriano en elocuencia,
Theodosio en humanidad
    y buen talante;
Aurelio Alexandre fue
en desciplina y rigor
    de la guerra;
un Costantino en la fe,
Camilo en el grand amor
    de su tierra.

[XXVIII]

Antonius Pius in his mercy;
Marcus Aurelius in the constancy
    of his mood;
Hadrian in eloquence;
Theodosius in humility
    and bright disposition;
Aurelius Alexandrus
in discipline and rigour
    in war;
in his faith, a Constantine;
Camillus in his great love
    for his land.

[XXIX]

No dexó grandes thesoros
ni alcancó grandes riquezas
    ni baxillas,
mas hizo guerra a los moros
ganando sus fortalezas
    y sus villas;
y en las lides que venció,
muchos moros y cavallos
    se perdieron,
y en este oficio ganó
las rentas y los vasallos
    que le dieron.

[XXIX]

He left no great treasures
amassed no great riches,
    or precious plate,
but he made war against the Moors,
conquering their fortresses
    and towns;
in the combats that he won
how many of their men and horses
    were cut down;
and this was how he gained
the vassals and the rents
    that passed to him.

[XXX]

Pues por su honra y estado,
en otros tiempos pasados,
   ¿cómo se uvo?
quedando desamparado,
con hermanos y criados
   se sostuvo.
Después que hechos famosos
hizo en esta dicha guerra
   que hazía,
hizo tratos tan honrosos
que le dieron aun más tierra
   que tenía.

[XXX]

    How did he fight
for his honour and his rank
      in earlier days?
When he was without protection,
with his brothers and his servants
      he stood firm.
After the great deeds he performed
in this war
      that he waged,
he made such honourable treaties
that more lands were added
      to those he had.

[XXXI]

Estas sus viejas estorias
que con su braço pintó
    en juventud,
con otras nuevas vitorias,
agora las renovó
    en senetud;
por su grand abilidad,
por méritos y ancianía
    bien gastada,
alcancó la dignidad
de la grand cavallería
    del espada.

[XXXI]

    These old scenes that he painted
with the strength of his arm
      when he was young,
he coloured them anew
with yet more victories
      when he was old.
Through his great skill,
his merits and his distinguished
      old age,
he attained the honour
of the knightly Order
      of the Sword.

[XXXII]

Y sus villas y sus tierras
ocupadas de tiranos
    las halló,
mas por cercos y por guerras
y por fuerca de sus manos
    las cobró.
Pues nuestro rey natural,
si de las obras que obró
    fue servído,
dígalo el de Portugal,
y en Castilla, quien siguió
    su partido.

[XXXII]

    And his towns and his lands
he found occupied
      by tyrants,
but with sieges and with wars,
and by the strength of his own hand,
      he regained them.
Thus if our rightful king
was well-served by the deeds
      he carried out,
let the king of Portugal admit as much;
and all those in Castile
      who took his side.

[XXXIII]

Después que puso la vida
tantas vezes por su ley
    al tablero,
después de tan bien servida
la corona de su rey
    verdadero,
después de tanta hazaña
a que no puede bastar
    cuenta cierta,
en la su villa de Ocaña,
vino la muerte a llamar
    a su puerta,

[XXXIII]

After having staked his life
so often in the cause
    of loyalty;
after having so well served
the crown of his true
    king,
after so many feats
that no mere number
    is enough to count them,
it was in his home town of Ocana
that Death came knocking
    on his door,

[XXXIV]

diziendo: —Buen cavallero,
dexad el mundo engañoso
   y su halago;
vuestro coracón de azero
muestre su esfuerce famoso
   en este trago.
Y pues de vida y salud
hezistes tan poca cuenta
   por la fama,
esfuércese la virtud
para sofrir esta afruenta
   que os llama.

[XXXIV]

    saying: 'Good knight,
leave this deceptive world
     and all its flattery;
your heart of steel must
show its famous mettle
     in this adversity;
for since you set so little store
by life and health
     for knightly fame,
draw strength from your virtue
as you suffer this affront
     that summons you.

[XXXV]

—No se os haga tan amarga
la batalla temerosa
    que esperáis,
pues otra vida más larga
de fama tan gloriosa
    acá dexáis;
aunque esta vida de honor
tampoco no es eternal
    ni verdadera,
mas con todo es muy mejor
que la otra temporal,
    perecedera.

[XXXV]

    Let not the fearful battle
that awaits
      be bitter to you,
for you leave behind you here
another, longer life of fame
      and glory.
And though this life of honour
is neither the eternal nor
      the true one;
it is, all told, far better
that that other, temporal life,
      that dies.

[XXXVI]

—El bevir que es perdurable
no se gana con estados
     mundanales
ni con vída deleitable
en que moran los pecados
     infernales;
mas los buenos religiosos
gánanlo con oraciones
     y con lloros,
los cavalleros famosos,
con trabajos y afliciones
     contra moros.

[XXXVI]

    The life that does not end
cannot be won with
      worldly things,
nor by a life of pleasures
where lie the sins
      of hell;
but it is won by pious men
through their prayers
      and their tears;
and by famous knights
through suffering and struggle
      against the Moors.

[XXXVII]

—Y pues vos, claro varón,
tanta sangre derramastes
   de paganos,
esperad el galardón
que en este mundo ganastes
   por las manos;
y con esta confiança
y con la fe tan entera
   que tenéis,
partid con buena esperança,
que esta otra vida tercera
   ganaréis.

[XXXVII]

And since you, illustrious warrior
spilled so much pagan
    blood,
you can look forward to the reward
that in this world and by your hands
    you won.
And with this certainty
and the unyielding faith
    you have,
depart in the sure hope
that you will win the third –
    eternal – life.'

[XXXVIII]

—No gastemos tiempo ya
en esta vida mezquina
      por tal modo,
que mi voluntad está
conforme con la divina
      para todo.
Y consiento en mi morir
con voluntad plazentera,
      clara y pura,
que querer ombre bivir
cuando Dios quiere que muera
      es locura.

[XXXVIII]

'Then let us not waste time
in this wretched life
    this way;
for my will is one
with the divine
    in everything;
and I consent to my dying
with joyful, pure and
    clear will;
for a man to wish to go on living
when God wishes that he die
    is madness.

[XXXIX]

—Tú, que por nuestra maldad
tomaste forma cevil
    y baxo nombre.
Tú, que a tu divinidad
juntaste cosa tan vil
    como es el ombre.
Tú, que tan grandes tormentos
sofriste sin resistencia
    en tu persona,
no por mis merescimientos,
mas por tu sola clemencia
    me perdona.

[XXXIX]

You, who, for our sins
took lowly form
    and humble name;
who joined to your divinity
a thing as vile
    as man;
you, who, unresisting, suffered
such cruel torments
    to your body,
grant me – not for my merits
but from your mercy only –
    Your forgiveness.

[XL]

Así, con tal entender,
todos sentidos humanos
    olvidados,
cercado de su muger
y de hijos y de hermanos
    y criados,
dio el alma a quien ge la dio,
el cual la ponga en el cielo
    y en su gloria;
y aunque la vida murió,
nos dexó harto consuelo
    su memoria.

[XL]

So, with this understanding,
all his human senses
    intact,
surrounded by his wife,
his children, his brothers
    and his servants,
he returned his soul to the God
who gave it to him;
may He raise it to heaven
    in its glory;
and though his life has ended,
he left us as our consolation
    his memory.

Translator's note

When I first read Manrique's *Coplas* I was drawn to its rhythm, to the universality of its subject, and to its mix of grandeur and plainness. It was as if I was being spoken to from somewhere at once far away and immediately close by. Reading the poem aloud and listening to its movement, I was struck by how well the utterances are shaped to the form they are given, how the longer lines allow a sense of expansion, of *élan*, while the shorter ones whittle them down, crop them, or cut them off altogether. This patterning makes for great variation amid the poem's overarching regularity, but since the metre, *pie quebrado*, or broken foot, is familiar to readers of Spanish poetry, and the poem's themes are canonical, there was nothing sophisticated about my response. I was simply noticing the obvious ways in which the poem's form and its content were perfectly aligned.

There is something reassuring in being excited about a poem that is neither new in its propositions nor particularly original in its execution: it reminds us that some works of art inhabit a space in which questions of precedence, or novelty, or originality (a modern concept anyway) are irrelevant. And as a reader, it can also be a relief to have the burden of coming up with an original response lifted; indeed that was a large part of the pleasure the poem gave me. I had nothing to offer to it but assent, and this is why I wanted to translate it: not just because I wanted to put it into English, but because translating it felt like a way of climbing inside it and assenting to it for a little longer.

I have tried to remain as close to Manrique's Spanish as possible, and hope that, whatever music this version has, it comes first of all from a fidelity to Manrique's words, which are as plain and unadorned as the feelings they give expression to. Robert Graves wrote that 'a true poem is best spoken in a level, natural voice: slowly or solemnly, and with a suppressed emotion'. This is how I hear Manrique, and how I have tried to convey him here. Since the leanness of his lines and the mattness of his diction are so important to the poem, I have resisted the temptation to embellish, or to add, or to turn up the volume with extra adverbs and adjectives. I have also respected the restricted palette of his vocabulary. Where I felt it worked in English and served both the original poem and my translation, I tried to follow Manrique's syntax, which in Spanish allows him to build up lengthy and multi-clausal sentences without losing the thread.

For a poem about death's universal and levelling dominion, it nonetheless contains a lot of information: people, battles, glories, riches and possessions are paraded before us, only for the poem to sweep them all away. The *ubi sunt* trope is compelling thanks to the energy of negative accumulation, the *going, going gone*-ness of things. Manrique's lists have a deadly relentlessness, mesmeric as well as chillingly deadpan, that relies on the sheer proliferation of examples: Romans, Trojans, Goths, Kings and Queens, Lords, Ladies, rich and poor... it is the world itself, in all its intricacy and interrelation, that shimmers before us in a dance of death. I have therefore kept the structure of Manrique's lists and their reiterations, though in one or two cases I have modernised and anglicised the names and titles of people.

A final comment about the metrical form: I have not chosen either to replicate the *pie quebrado* or to find an equivalent English form. The idea of 'equivalent form', were it even possible, seems to me to create as many problems as it tries to resolve. I preferred to keep, in a diluted but nonetheless perceptible way, a sense of Manrique's original rhythm. I have also sacrificed Manrique's tight rhyme scheme, so punchily effective in the original, but tried to make up for it, in part, through internal rhyme and sound-patterning, albeit in ways that are unsystematic.

Acknowledgments

I'd like to thank my friend and colleague Geraldine Hazbun for her introduction and for many discussions of Manrique's poem. David Hook gave me invaluable help on matters both general and specific, and I'm grateful for his generosity, precision and tact.

Patrick McGuinness is Professor of French and Comparative Literature at Oxford, and Sir Win and Lady Bishoff Fellow in French at St Anne's College. He works on modern literature in French, as well as British and American poetry. His books include two volumes of poetry, two novels, and translations from a number of writers, including Mallarmé, Hélène Dorion and Gilles Ortlieb. His most recent books are a novel, *Throw Me to the Wolves* (2019), and *Real Oxford* (2021), an exploration of the city behind the dreaming spires.

www.ingramcontent.com/pod-product-compliance
Ingram Content Group UK Ltd.
Pitfield, Milton Keynes, MK11 3LW, UK
UKHW041433241224
3859UKWH00044B/271